Walter Johnson

THE STORY OF THE WASHINGTON NATIONALS

Third baseman Anthony Rendon

THE STORY OF THE

WASHINGTON NATIONALS

MICHAEL E. GOODMAN

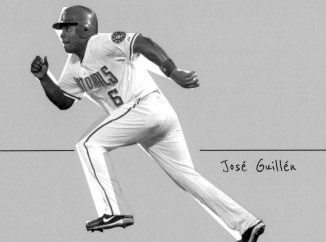

José Guillén

CREATIVE EDUCATION / CREATIVE PAPERBACKS

Published by Creative Education and Creative Paperbacks
P.O. Box 227, Mankato, Minnesota 56002
Creative Education and Creative Paperbacks are imprints of The Creative Company
www.thecreativecompany.us

Design and production by Blue Design (www.bluedes.com)
Art direction by Rita Marshall
Printed in China

Photographs by Alamy (Tim Brown, Cal Sport Media, UPI, Harry E. Walker/
MCT/Tribune Content Agency LLC), Corbis (Bettmann), Getty Images (Al Bello/
Allsport, Andrew D. Bernstein, Lisa Blumenfeld, David Boily/MLB Photos,
Ricky Carioti/The Washington Post, Kevin C. Cox, Diamond Images, Stephen
Dunn, G Fiume, Focus on Sport, David L. Greene/MLB Photos, Paul Jasienski,
Jonathan Kirn/Allsport, Mitchell Layton, Mitchell Layton/MLB Photos, John
McDonnell/The Washington Post, National Baseball Hall of Fame Library,
National Baseball Hall of Fame Library/MLB Photos, Christian Petersen, Rich
Pilling/MLB Photos, Joe Robbins, Robert Skeoch/MLB Photos, Don Smith/MLB
Photos, Jamie Squire, Ron Vesely/MLB Photos)

Library of Congress Cataloging-in-Publication Data
Names: Goodman, Michael E., author.
Title: Washington Nationals / Michael E. Goodman.
Series: Creative sports. Veterans.
Includes index.
Summary: Encompassing the extraordinary history of Major League Baseball's
Washington Nationals, this photo-laden narrative underscores significant
players, team accomplishments, and noteworthy moments that will stand
out in young sports fans' minds.
Identifiers: ISBN 978-1-64026-323-9 (hardcover) / ISBN 978-1-62832-855-4
(pbk) / ISBN 978-1-64000-453-5 (eBook)
This title has been submitted for CIP processing under LCCN 2020901779.

First Edition HC 9 8 7 6 5 4 3 2 1
First Edition PBK 9 8 7 6 5 4 3 2 1

Outfielder Moisés Alou

CONTENTS

EXTRA INNINGS

CANADIAN ROOTS

A buzz filled Nationals Park in Washington, D.C., on June 8, 2010. Christmas was more than six months away, but local writers and fans called this night "Strasmas." Rookie pitching sensation Stephen Strasburg was making his major-league debut in a Washington Nationals uniform. Strasburg's first pitch flew past Pittsburgh's hitter at 98 miles per hour. Over seven innings, Strasburg mowed down one Pirates batter after another. He finished with 14 strikeouts, a new Nationals record. He also earned the first of his many victories as a Washington player. For fans, the night promised a bright future for the team in the nation's capital.

Baseball is sometimes called America's pastime. As such, it would seem fitting for there to be a Major League Baseball (MLB) team in the country's capital. However, Washington, D.C., has had a hard time keeping baseball teams. In the 1880s and '90s, two different D.C. teams played in the National League (NL). Neither lasted long. In 1901, the Washington Senators team was established in the newly formed American League (AL). This franchise stayed put for 60 seasons. Then it moved to Minnesota and became the Twins. The following year, another Senators franchise replaced the one that had moved away. It relocated to Texas before the 1972 season. There, it became the Rangers.

Washington baseball fans had no home team from 1972 through 2004. Farther north, the Montreal Expos were having financial problems. The NL decided to move

Pitcher Stephen Strasburg

EXTRA INNINGS

OLYMPIC STADIUM,
MONTREAL, QUEBEC,
SEPTEMBER 6, 1993

CANADA DAY?

It was a special day for Canadian baseball fans. For the first time, the Expos' starting lineup featured three Canadian-born players. All-Star Larry Walker (pictured) was in right field. Two new Expos players, Joe Siddall and Denis Boucher, were the starting catcher and pitcher. Fans packed the stadium. Many came to see Boucher, who was from nearby Lachine, Quebec. They gave a standing ovation when his name was announced. They kept cheering when Walker hit a home run. Fans gave Boucher another ovation when he left the game after six strong innings. In the eighth, Siddall helped power the Expos to the win.

the club to D.C. to become the Nationals in 2005. It took a few years to adjust to its new location. Soon, the Nationals had a competitive ballclub and a solid fan base.

Before becoming the Nationals, the Expos had enjoyed 36 seasons in Montreal, Quebec. The team had been established during the MLB expansion of 1969. Its name came from an impressive world's fair held two years earlier in Montreal. This was commonly referred to as Expo 67. The Expos were an immediate hit with French-speaking Montreal fans. They called the players "Nos Amours" (our loves).

The Expos built their first roster through an expansion draft. They selected young unknowns and aging veterans from the other NL teams. Among their picks were pitcher Bill Stoneman, third baseman Coco Laboy, and second baseman Gary Sutherland. But the team lacked star power. Management decided to make a key trade before the Expos played their first season. They sent several players to the Houston Astros. In return, they received hard-hitting right fielder Rusty Staub. His fiery red hair earned him the nickname "Le Grand Orange." His outgoing nature made him an instant hero in Montreal.

Le Grand Orange and the Expos kicked off their first season with a dramatic flair. They faced the Mets in New York on April 8. Laboy, Staub, and relief pitcher Dan McGinn all belted home runs. The big hits led to a wild 11–10 Opening-Day win. The team played its home opener in rickety Jarry Park a week later. It won that game, too. Three nights later, Stoneman tossed a no-hitter against the Philadelphia Phillies.

Still, like most expansion teams, the Expos struggled. They finished the year with a 52–110 record. They made solid improvements over the next few years. Montreal fans continued filling the stands in Jarry Park. In 1977, the club moved to the larger, more modern Olympic Stadium. Players and fans looked forward to good times ahead.

BUILDING A WINNER

The Expos built a solid minor-league system to train talented young players for the big leagues. One of the first to make his way north was third baseman Larry Parrish in 1974. He was a solid clutch hitter. Right fielder/catcher Gary Carter arrived soon after. He was nicknamed "Kid." He had youthful looks and enthusiasm, but he possessed grown-up talent. In 1975, he was named to the All-Star team. Before his career was over, Carter made 10 more All-Star appearances. Eventually, he entered the Hall of Fame.

Carter's career took an upward turn in 1977. Manager Dick Williams named him the Expos' full-time catcher. Carter established himself as a steady leader on the field. He also blossomed as a hitter. That year, he averaged .284 with 31 homers and 84 runs batted in (RBI). Rookie Andre Dawson took over in the outfield. He patrolled center field like a giant bird of prey. He became known as "The Hawk." Dawson finished the season with 19 homers and 21 stolen bases. His performance earned him the NL Rookie of the Year award.

Led by their young stars, the Expos steadily climbed the NL East Division ladder. They reached second place in 1979. It was the team's first winning season. Montreal fans began chanting, "Vive les Expos" (Long live the Expos). They hoped the next season would include a championship run.

Montreal jumped to a quick start in 1980. Carter, Dawson, and Parrish led the high-powered offense. Pitchers Steve Rogers and Scott Sanderson dominated

Right fielder Rusty Staub

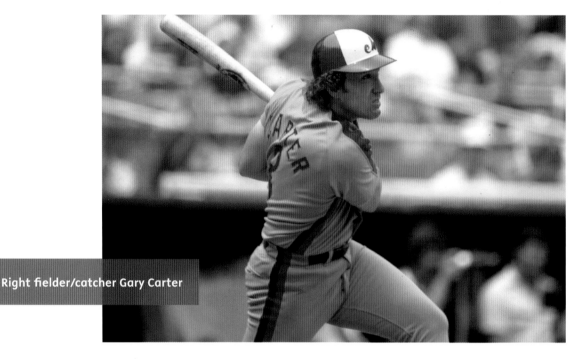

Right fielder/catcher Gary Carter

the mound. The Expos went into the final weekend of the season in a close race with the Phillies for the division lead. The rivals faced off in a three-game series. Philadelphia won twice. Montreal's postseason ambitions ended.

The Expos gunned for the playoffs again in 1981. Rookie sensation Tim Raines joined the lineup. The young left fielder was an excellent leadoff hitter and base stealer. A players' strike divided the 1981 season into two halves. Philadelphia won the first half of the season. In the second half, the Expos posted the best record in the division. They defeated the Phillies in a special playoff series.

Montreal then faced the Los Angeles Dodgers in the NL Championship Series (NLCS). The teams split the first four games. A snowstorm postponed the deciding Game 5 until Monday, October 19. It was a tight matchup. The score was tied in the ninth inning. Manager Jim Fanning summoned Rogers from the bullpen to shut down the Dodgers. Unfortunately, Dodgers outfielder Rick Monday hit a slider out of the park. With that, Los Angeles won the NLCS. Expos fans were left to sadly reflect on "Blue Monday."

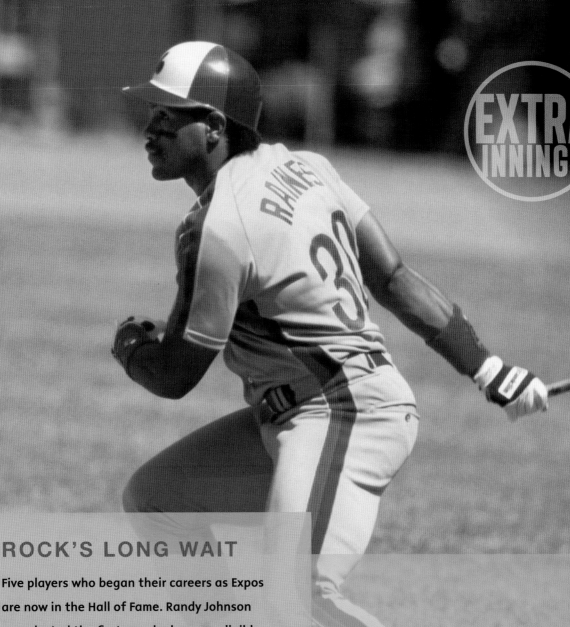

ROCK'S LONG WAIT

Five players who began their careers as Expos
are now in the Hall of Fame. Randy Johnson
was elected the first year he became eligible.
Vladimir Guerrero took two years. Andre Dawson
and Gary Carter took longer to attain the 75
percent of the votes needed for election to the
Hall. For Tim Raines, the wait was even longer.
"Rock" finally made it in 2017. It was his 10th
and final year of eligibility. Raines played 13 of
his 23 seasons in Montreal. As of 2019, he led
the franchise in stolen bases (635), runs scored
(947), triples (82), and walks (793).

WASHINGTON NATIONALS

15

Thomas Jefferson, Theodore Roosevelt, Abraham Lincoln, and George Washington

THE PRESIDENTS' RACE

During the fourth inning of every Nationals home game, runners wearing foam heads of former presidents race to the cheers of fans. Starting in 2006, racers dressed as George Washington, Abraham Lincoln, Thomas Jefferson, and Theodore Roosevelt. Over the first few years, there was never a consistent winner. But there was a consistent loser—Teddy Roosevelt. Race after race, he would lose or get disqualified. After a while, some fans began to chant, "Let Teddy win!" They finally got their wish in the last home game of 2012. Teddy's opponents were knocked down during the race. He crossed the finish line first, victorious at last!

THE ROAD TO D.C.

The Expos stayed competitive. But they could not get back to the playoffs. Montreal featured many outstanding players. In 1982, first baseman Al Oliver hit .331. He was the first Expos player to win the NL batting title. Fireballing pitcher Jeff Reardon began a string of impressive seasons as the team's closer. He was the top reliever in the major leagues in 1985. Third baseman Tim Wallach was a doubles machine. He also won three Gold Glove awards for his fielding. Raines continued to steal bases and slash hits. In 1986, he led the NL with a .334 batting average.

The team's roster underwent several key changes during the 1980s. Carter was traded away. Dawson left as a free agent. New stars such as first baseman Andrés Galarraga and pitcher Dennis Martínez emerged as team leaders. Despite their efforts, Montreal's record hovered near .500 into the 1990s.

In 1994, fans sensed that something special was finally happening. After a solid start, the team posted an eight-game winning streak in July. It topped the NL East from then on out. By early August, the Expos held a seven game lead. They were powered by outfielders Moisés Alou and Larry Walker at the plate. Wily young Pedro Martínez controlled the mound. Expos fans dreamed of a championship. They were rudely awakened on August 12. Major-league players went on strike. Fruitless negotiations dragged on for weeks. Then the season was canceled. The finest team in franchise history would not have the chance to prove itself in the

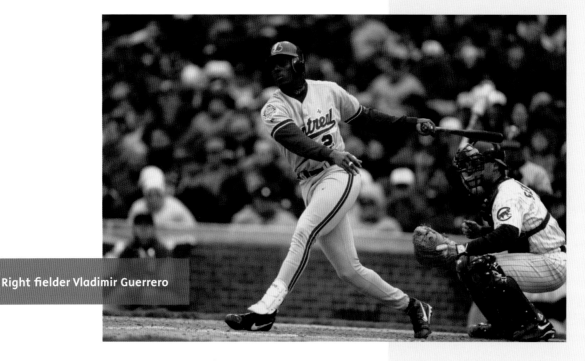

Right fielder Vladimir Guerrero

postseason. "A lot of things about the strike hurt," Walker said. "But having that great season wasted is something I don't think I'll ever get over."

The depressing end to the 1994 season deflated the team. But fans were still excited to see Pedro Martínez pitch. He rewarded their loyalty by winning the Cy Young Award in 1997. Right fielder Vladimir Guerrero was another outstanding talent. He had a quick bat, speed, and an amazing throwing arm. Guerrero earned four All-Star appearances and three Silver Slugger awards as an Expos player.

By the early 2000s, many fans had stopped coming to Olympic Stadium. Rumors suggested that the MLB might eliminate the Expos. Instead, the league began to search for new owners and a new home. Several cities vied for the franchise. Las Vegas, Nevada, and Portland, Oregon, expressed interest. Monterrey, Mexico, was even a possibility. In the end, team ownership went to a group in Washington, D.C. In 2004, city leaders announced the good news. "After 30 years of waiting and waiting and waiting," said mayor Anthony Williams, "and lots of hard work and more than a few prayers, there will be baseball in Washington in 2005!"

Pitcher Pedro Martinez

NO-NOS

Max Scherzer tossed a no-hitter against the Mets on October 3, 2015. It was his second of the year. He became only the sixth pitcher in major-league history to throw two no-hitters in the same season. Scherzer joined a short list of Expos/Nationals pitchers who have thrown no-nos. Bill Stoneman no-hit the Phillies in April 1969. He hurled a second no-no in October 1972. Nine years later, Charlie Lea tossed a no-hitter. Dennis Martínez (pictured) threw an impressive game on July 28, 1991. He did not allow any Dodgers players to reach base. The perfect game ended in a 2–0 win. Jordan Zimmermann threw the team's first no-no in Washington, D.C., in 2014.

CAPITAL EXCITEMENT

Baseball's return to the U.S. capital was a resounding success. It had been 34 years since the Senators had left Washington for Texas. The city's baseball-starved citizens were ready to embrace the team. More than 2.7 million fans passed through the turnstiles at Robert F. Kennedy Stadium in 2005. Fewer than 750,000 had attended games the year before in Montreal.

Players quickly endeared themselves to fans. Pitcher Liván Hernández won 15 games. He led the majors in innings pitched. Right fielder José Guillén smacked 24 home runs. Closer Chad Cordero recorded an MLB-leading 47 saves. Now known as the Nationals, the team finished the season with a respectable 81–81 record.

Over the next few seasons, several veteran players signed on. These included outfielders Austin Kearns and Alfonso Soriano and infielders Dmitri Young and Ronnie Belliard. But the Nationals' offense struggled. One true star did emerge during this period. Ryan Zimmerman became the team's starting third baseman in 2006. He took over the third spot in the batting lineup. Zimmerman soon established himself as the team's best run producer and top fielder.

Big changes were already in the wind. In 2007, a new group of owners took over. Stan Kasten was brought in as team president. He introduced "The Plan" for rebuilding and restructuring every aspect of the franchise. One of the first big steps was moving the team to a new home in 2008. Nationals Park, along the Anacostia River in southeast Washington, D.C., offered sightlines of many D.C.

landmarks. It also provided great views of the on-field action. The new stadium was one of the country's most environmentally friendly sports structures.

Fans packed the stands for the first game at Nationals Park. President George W. Bush threw out the ceremonial first pitch. Zimmerman hit a walk-off homer to cap a thrilling 3–2 victory. Unfortunately, that game proved to be a rare highlight. Injuries plagued the team. It won only 59 games. In 2009, Zimmerman led the "Nats" with 106 RBI. He was named to the All-Star team. Despite his success, the Nationals again tallied just 59 wins.

There was a silver lining to these poor finishes. The Nationals were awarded the first overall pick in the MLB Draft. They used their 2009 and 2010 picks to select two outstanding prospects. One was Stephen Strasburg. In college, his fastball regularly topped 100 miles per hour. "Whenever you see a fastball at 100 miles per hour, it's always straight. No movement," noted one scout. "But his fastball cuts." The other draftee was hard-hitting teenage outfielder Bryce Harper. He had played both outfielder and catcher in high school. *Sports Illustrated* described him as the best teenage power-hitting prospect since Mickey Mantle. Fans cheered both selections. They looked forward to watching the new players perform at Nationals Park.

Third baseman Ryan Zimmerman

NATIONALS PARK

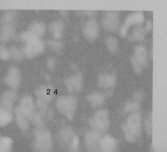

A GREEN BALLPARK

When Nationals Park opened in 2008, the field was not the only "green" thing. The ballpark was built to be environmentally friendly. High-efficiency lighting uses less electricity. Much of the stadium's power is generated by solar panels. Water is carefully filtered to make sure no pollution flows into the nearby Anacostia River. Lawn mowers and field maintenance vehicles are also extra efficient. Most vehicles used inside the stadium are electric. Even the cleaning supplies are environmentally responsible. Nationals management believes that a great team needs a special home.

WASHINGTON WINNERS

By 2012, Strasburg and Harper were in place. They joined several other key draft picks and free agents. Among those players were catcher Wilson Ramos, shortstop Ian Desmond, second baseman Danny Espinosa, and pitcher Gio González. Veteran manager Davey Johnson took the reins. He promised to lead the team into the postseason.

Many people believed the 2012 roster possessed a special quality. They called it "Natitude." As team executive Andy Feffer explained, "It's a young team, with an edge and attitude…. They're talented, and they've got the skills to back it up. That kind of edge and attitude is Natitude."

González topped the majors with 21 wins. Strasburg added 15. Zimmerman and first baseman Adam LaRoche led the team in homers and RBI. The Nationals finished the season with 98 wins. The highly anticipated postseason was filled with excitement. But the NL Division Series (NLDS) ended poorly for Washington. The Nationals and the St. Louis Cardinals split the first four games of the series. Washington jumped out to a 6–0 lead in the deciding Game 5. But St. Louis rallied to win. The Nationals' championship dreams were over.

The Nats were back in the postseason two years later. They had a new standout. Third baseman Anthony Rendon was a solid fielder. He was an even better hitter. He won a Silver Slugger award in 2014 and pounded out 39 doubles. Sportswriters dubbed him "Tony Two-Bags." (True to his nickname, Rendon would

NATIONALS PARK,
WASHINGTON, D.C.,
JULY 27, 2017

HOMER DAY

The weather was warm on July 27, 2017. But there was no power
outage at Nationals Park. In the bottom of the third inning
against the Milwaukee Brewers, Brian Goodwin smacked a
two-run homer. Next, Wilmer Difo, Bryce Harper, and Ryan
Zimmerman took turns at bat. They all homered. That tied
an MLB record for consecutive home runs. After a one-batter
pause, Anthony Rendon also hit a moonshot. That meant
Washington tallied five dingers in a single inning! In all, the
Nationals slugged eight homers in a 15–2 rout of the Brewers.

Shortstop Ian Desmond

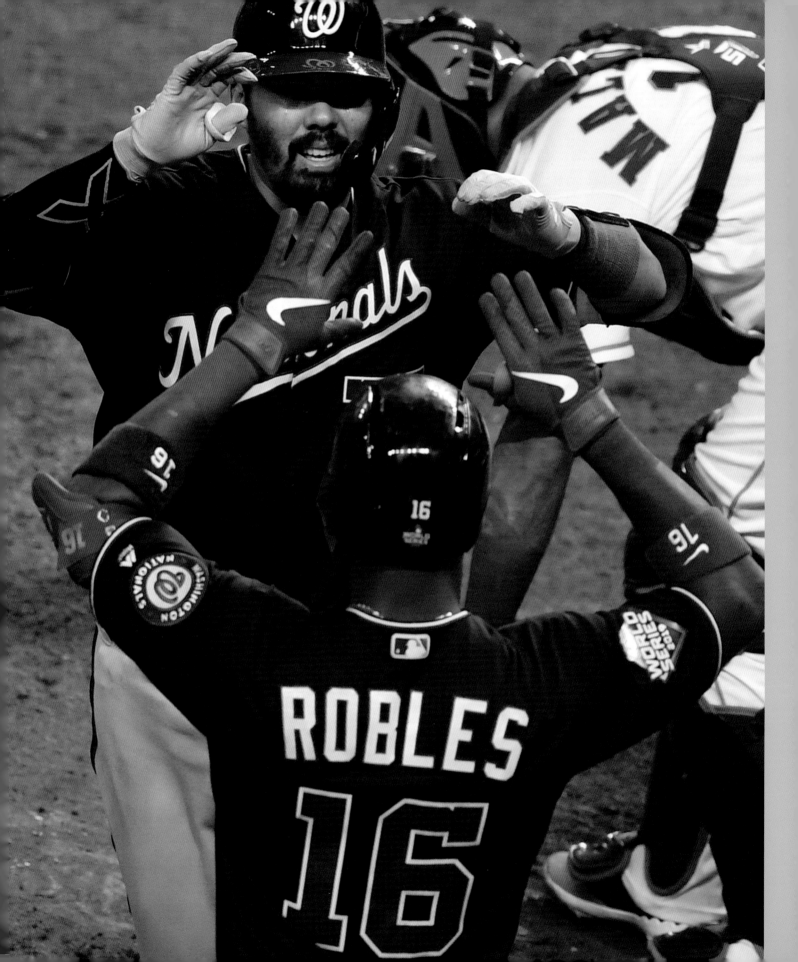

lead the NL in doubles in 2018 and 2019. He also topped the major leagues with 126 RBI in 2019.)

Washington failed to move beyond the NLDS in 2014. It suffered the same fate in 2016 and 2017. But it continued to retool and improve. The team added Cy Young Award-winning pitcher Max Scherzer. Speedy infielder Trea Turner and teenage Dominican left fielder Juan Soto also came onboard.

In 2019, the Nationals made history. After falling 12 games below .500 early in the season, they hit an impressive winning streak. They earned a Wild Card berth. In the playoffs, they took care of the Milwaukee Brewers. Then they met the Dodgers in the dreaded NLDS. This time, the Nats won the deciding game thanks to a 10th inning grand slam by second sacker Howie Kendrick.

That was just the start. The Nationals swept the Cardinals in the NLCS to reach the World Series for the first time in franchise history. Then, in one of the most dramatic World Series ever, Washington trailed in six of the games. It roared back to win three of those contests. The Nationals stunned Houston by pushing the "Fall Classic" to seven games. They overpowered the Astros to win the final game. At last, they were the world champions! During the postgame celebration, Scherzer and fellow pitcher Aníbal Sánchez embraced and cried. "We finally won one!" Sánchez exclaimed.

For Expos and Nationals fans, many postseason battles had ended in disappointment. Now, fans hoped the team's 2019 championship was a beacon of great things to come. The franchise's history spans two countries and includes players and fans from many different cultures. As one sportswriter suggested, "Maybe they should really be called the Washington Internationals."

Catcher Kurt Suzuki and Center fielder Víctor Robles

INDEX